The Metabolic Typing ® Cookbook
For 1-O, Slow Oxidation
Eating to live, not living to eat

Nancy Dale C.N.

Forward by William Wolcott author of
The Metabolic Typing® Diet

Gluten Free....

For the past ten to twenty years I have seen in my practice a steady increase in the amount of gluten sensitivity with my clients. I am not talking about celiac disease which is a very dangerous and serious disorder that makes a person allergic to gluten (wheat, oats, barley or rye). I am seeing two thirds of my clients come in complaining of weight gain, fatigue, sleep disorders, bloating, gas, high blood sugar and uncontrollable cravings., just to name a few.

When I have suggested that they take "gluten" out of their diet for just one week to see how they feel the results have been amazing. From losing two to four pounds in just one week and having more energy and a flatter stomach to even sleeping better. I am convinced that we can and quite possibly, should live without gluten.

That does not mean to live without carbohydrates. We need fiber and eating vegetables and fruits is the best way to assure that we get enough fiber in out diet. I also recommend the non-gluten grains such as brown rice, quinoa, millet, amaranth and wild rice.

I do not recommend most of the "new" gluten free products that have been created. Most of these products are filled with ingredients that are highly processed and should not be ingested. Especially if you are trying to lose some weight or lower your blood sugars.

For this reason I have created a gluten free version of my cookbooks. If you would like more information on this subject I recommend reading Wheat Belly by William Davis, MD and also the book Grain Brain by David Perlmutter, MD.

Nancy Dale C.N.
Winter 2013

Credits

The Metabolic Typing ® Cookbook for 1-O, Slow Oxidation

Gluten Free Copyright © 2013 Nancy Dale
Copyright © 2010 by Nancy Dale

No part of this book may be used
or reproduced in any manner whatsoever without
prior written permission from the publisher.

Text and Recipes by Nancy Dale, C.N.
Book Design: Nancy Dale C.N. and Meg Fish Photography
Photography: Meg Fish Photography

All Rights Reserved

ISBN 978-0-9827385-6-6

To order this and the other five Metabolic Typing® Cookbooks
Visit us on the web: www.nancydalecn.com

Contents

preface 5
forward 6
acknowledgment 7
introduction 8

glycemic index 10
facts on fiber 12
emotional eating 13
metabolic type 14
foods for your type 15
shopping list 16

begin the day 19
salads and more 31
soups and one pot meals 45
vegetables and more 67
proteins 75
desserts and snacks 101

glossary 113
legend, weight and measures 117
index 119
resources 123

Eating to live, not living to eat.

Preface

This book took over fifteen years to create and I believe it is still a work in progress. I began cooking when I was a small girl. When I became a certified nutritionist I decided to delve into cooking from a health standpoint. Just as I completed my chef certificate in 1994 my mother was diagnosed with liver cancer. I quickly moved in with her and began cooking as a means to bring her back to health. She was given just weeks to live. I lived with her for 5 ½ years cooking all the while.

At that same time I started my clinical nutrition practice. I could only work part time while attending to my mother. I started cooking for my clients to show them what healthy meals taste like and before long I had developed a business of creating healthy meals, delivered to my clients. I lived in the Southern California area and began working with the movie industry. I was hired to work with the stars when their role required them to lose weight or to get healthier. Most of the meals in this book were created at that time.

Since moving to the Santa Barbara area I no longer cook and deliver my food. I now teach cooking classes in my home twice a year and operate two nutrition offices.

I became a Certified Metabolic Typing ® Advisor five years ago and began creating menus based on that same principle.

All of the recipes in the book have been created with your health in mind. We can not expect restaurants or prepared foods to give us health. It is my hope that you begin to love cooking as much as I do.

Bon appétit!

Nancy Dale C.N., CMTA, FDN

Foreword

Over 30 years ago, my sojourn with Metabolic Typing® first began. From the very first encounter, I knew in my heart, in my whole being, that I had been blessed with the good fortune to have found something very special. So intriguing, so rewarding has that 3 decades long journey been, that nothing has been able to entice my one-pointed attention away from my quest to uncover the wondrous and amazing secrets of health possible through Metabolic Typing®.

As might be imagined, a lot can happen over 3 decades – or over half a lifetime in my case. And so it has. Just like the accidental discovery of a piece of a broken pot can lead to an anthropological dig that unearths an entire ancient city, what began as a one dimensional concept to determine individual dietary requirements has evolved, one discovery at a time, into an 11 dimensional model for the science of optimal health known as Metabolic Typing®.

The complexity, depth and breadth of this scientific discipline is staggering, when understood in its entirety. And yet, the day-to-day application of the truths revealed through Metabolic Typing® is utterly simple, once you know exactly what to do and how to do it.

Through the Metabolic Typing® Cookbooks, Nancy Dale has provided what may indeed be the most important tool for successfully living the "metabolic typing lifestyle." Nancy's hard won and heartfelt contribution to all of us in the form of the Metabolic Typing® Cookbooks is a natural expression of that rare, priceless combination of time, talent and experience, combined with a giving nature and a loving heart.

The world is rife with so-called experts. These days, anyone can write a book, self-publish it on the internet and with a little marketing savvy, appear authoritative. But the truth is that which lasts longest. And it is as true today as it has been since time immemorial, that expertise is possible only from the knowledge and understanding born from experience. Nancy Dale has an abundance of both.

Nancy has been one of the most active Certified Metabolic Typing® Advisors in the world over the last 5 years and her thriving, extremely successful practice with hundreds of enthusiastic, happy clients is testament to her expertise. Nancy's background as a successful, professional chef, combined with her extensive clinical experience with Metabolic Typing® makes her uniquely qualified to author these cookbooks. We are all fortunate to have them, myself included!

Read them. Use them. And enjoy the energy, well-being and good health that surely will ensue!

William L. Wolcott
Author, The Metabolic Typing® Diet (Doubleday, 2000)
Winthrop, Washington, December, 2009

Acknowledgement

This has been the most rewarding project I have ever worked on. This book along with the other five metabolic typing ® cookbooks has been a labor of love.

The bulk of the recipes were created from teaching my cooking classes throughout the years. It was not until 2009 that I actually fine-tuned the recipes to have only the ingredients for each particular type for each recipe- not an easy task when you consider each recipe must be created using only those ingredients.

A special thanks to Meg Fish for her amazing photography and her special artistic touch seen throughout the books; Neither one of us had ever edited or created a book before so it was a pleasure to have someone so full of energy and enthusiasm to work with.

I would also like to acknowledge Bill Wolcott for his wonderful support and encouragement. Without him we would not have this incredible metabolic typing ® approach to health.

To all my students and clients who have tasted my recipes and to all of you who are about to try them; I hope you like them as much as I do.

Eating to Live, not living to eat,

Nancy Dale

Introduction

These recipes are meant to be a starting point; adding more or less of any of the proteins, fats and carbohydrates until you feel satisfied. Experiment; this is how I created these recipes with the intent of customizing to fit your needs.

Most of the recipes are for multiple meals. I actually cook on Sunday for all week. I choose what recipes I am going to make and create a shopping list of ingredients a day or two prior to cooking. I involve everyone in the fun of choosing what they would like to eat. On the week-end I reserve a couple of hours to cook all of the meals for the upcoming week.

When the food has cooled, I divide each portion so that each person has the right amount to begin with.

It is a complete delight for me to walk into my kitchen at the end of a long day and open my refrigerator to any number of meals I have made that can be easily re-heated in the oven or on the stove top. In minutes we are sitting down to a great home cooked meal. This can also be very important if you have multiple Metabolic Types® in one family.

I generally steam different vegetables that can be eaten by all as well. When I am making poultry I try to have dark meat as well as breast.

Having multiple meals at your finger tip will help to keep everyone eating the right foods for their Metabolic Type ®.

- If you have food sensitivities omit the offending food that you have reactions to or substitute with another food from the same macronutrient group. Example: Instead of asparagus use cauliflower. Instead of salmon use halibut.

- If you have weight issues try to eat less at each meal by a mouthful or two. Wait twenty minutes and see if you are comfortable. This is what I call "mindfully under eating".

- Eat sitting down at a table without distractions from the TV or computer. Never eat standing up or in your car.

- Do not eat if you are really stressed. Instead have a glass of water relax for a few minutes and wait until you have calmed down.

- Sweeteners such as stevia can be exchanged for xylitol, maple syrup, organic pure cane sugar or fruit juice, but use less of them and taste for sweetness, (less is better). You may substitute honey only in the dishes that do not require cooking, such as the yogurt or protein smoothies.

- Remember after each meal or snack you should feel satisfied, have great energy, have a sense of feeling renewed and restored. You should not have food cravings or a desire for more food. If you have any bad reactions such as feeling full, but still hungry or hyper, jittery you need to make sure you ate the right amount of protein, fats and carbohydrates for your type. An example of this might be at breakfast eating eggs makes you sluggish. Try having a protein smoothie and see if that makes you feel more energized. This is what this whole process is about. Learning exactly what fuel works in each body at each meal. For additional help please contact your Metabolic Typing ® advisor to help you fine-tune this process.

Glycemic Index

Grains

Corn bread	110	Stoned wheat thins	67
Instant rice	91	Quick Oats	65
Corn chips	72	Basmati white rice	58
Millet	71	Whole wheat pita	57
Corn tortilla	70	White rice	56
Corn meal	68	Corn	55
Rye crackers	68	Oatmeal, old fashioned	48
Taco shell	68	Bulgur	48
Couscous	65	Barley	25

Bread

French baguette	95	Hamburger bun	61
Pretzels	81	Cheese pizza	60
Kaiser roll	73	Bran muffin	60
Bagel	72	Blueberry muffin	60
White bread	70	Pita	57
Melba toast	70	Sourdough	54
Whole wheat	69	Oat bran	54
Rye	65	Banana	47
Croissant	67	Pumpernickel	41

Pasta

Linguine	55	Vermicelli	35
Cheese Tortellini	50	Spaghetti	35
Macaroni	45	Fettuccini	32
Spaghetti	44	Spaghetti (protein enrich)	28
" " whole wheat	37		

Beverages

Gaterade	78	Grapefruit juice	51
Cranberry juice	68	Pineapple juice	48
Coca cola	63	Apple juice	41
Orange juice	55	Tomato juice	38

Dairy

Yogurt with fruit	36	Yogurt	14
Milk (fat free)	32	Whole milk	30
Cottage cheese	24		

Fruit

Watermelon	72	Orange	43
Pineapple	66	Grapes	43

Fruits, Cont.

Cantaloupe	65	Strawberries	40
Raisins	64	Apple	36
Apricot	31	Pear	36
Papaya	60	Peaches	28
Banana	53	Plum	24
Kiwi	52	Grapefruit	25
Date	50	Cherries	22

Potato

Potato	104	Mashed potato	73
Red potato	93	Potato chips	54
Instant mashed	83	Sweet potato	54
French fries	76	Yam	51

Legumes

Pea soup	66	Lima beans	32
Split pea and ham	66	Chick peas	32
Black beans	54	Navy beans	31
Butter beans	36	Lentils	30
Black eyed peas	42	Kidneys	23
Garbanzo	34	Peanuts	13
Beans(string/ green)	0		

Nuts

Cashews	22	Macadamia	0
Almonds	0	Pecans	0
Brazil	0	Walnuts	0
Hazelnuts	0		

Vegetables

Carrots	92	Eggplant	0
Beets	64	Snow peas	0
Tomato	15	Artichoke	0
Mushroom	0	Peppers	0
Broccoli	0	Asparagus	0
Cauliflower	0	Zucchini	0
Cabbage	0	Cucumber	0
Celery	0	Lettuce	0

Meat/Protein

Beef	0	Lamb	0
Chicken	0	Pork	0
Eggs	0	Fish	0

Try to keep most of your choices below "40"

Facts on Fiber

What does fiber do? There are two types of fiber: insoluble (the kind found in vegetables, wheat and whole grains) and soluble (the kind found in fruits, oats, barley and legumes).

Insoluble fiber seems to fight cancer by binding to or diluting cancer-causing agents in the gut and speeding them through the colon.

Soluble fiber has its own part to play in keeping the body healthy: preventing heart disease. This kind of fiber forms a gel in the intestines that traps and ushers cholesterol out of the body. Soluble fiber can help reduce insulin levels, which in turn lowers triglycerides.

High fiber diets slow down the rate of digestion, which lowers both blood sugar levels and the insulin needed to transport that blood sugar into the cells.

Foods high in soluble fiber stay in your stomach longer creating a feeling of fullness that lasts longer so you eat less. Eating a diet high in soluble fiber will allow you to lose an average of 1/2 pound per week.

Food	Fiber (grams)
wheat-bran cereal (1/2 cup)	11
oatmeal (1 cup cooked)	4
brown rice (1 cup)	3.5
barley (1/2 cup cooked)	3
whole wheat bread	2
potato (baked with skin on)	5
carrots (1/2 cup cooked)	3
Brussels sprouts (1/2 cup cooked)	2.5
black-eyed peas (1/2 cups cooked)	8
black beans (1/2 cup cooked)	7.5
kidney beans (1/2 cup cooked)	6.5
lima beans (1/2 cup cooked)	6.5
apple (with skin on)	4
pear (with skin on)	4
raisins (2/3 cup seedless)	4
raspberries (1/2 cup)	4
orange (1 medium)	3.5

Boosting your fiber intake to the recommended 25-35 grams a day is good for your health. It can cause excess gas and be tough on your stomach. Here are some tips to ease the discomfort.

Go slowly. Increase your fiber by 5 grams per week.

Think small. Eat smaller portions of problematic foods such as beans and whole grains. Eat fruit that contain insoluble fiber which are easier to digest.

Emotional Eating

You are continually nourished by the world around you. When you close yourself to that nutrition, you feel the need to provide it yourself.

That is when food becomes magnetic. You do not have the capacity to provide yourself with the nourishment that you crave, and so eating becomes endless. It is not the calories you seek, but contact with your soul (going home) and with the universe. That is where true satisfaction exists, and is complete, nourishing and sustains life. No amount of chocolate, chips, salsa, macaroni and cheese can substitute for this.

You can not receive too much nourishment from the universe any more than you can breathe too much air. When you do not have enough air, you gasp. When you do not have enough nourishment of your soul you seek substitution in food. You can eat too much food.

Eating more than you need is not necessarily a sign of a chemical imbalance or eating the wrong types of food. It is a sign that you are fundamentally out of balance. Until that correction is made, compulsive hunger will continue to remind you that you have inner work to do. It is a gift; gentle reminders to pay attention to what is going on in your world and make the corrections to create a healthy body, mind and spirit.

Dieting and exercise cannot reach the root of obsessive eating. Eating the right foods in the right amounts and exercising are prerequisites for physical health. However, illnesses are symptoms of deeper dynamics that bear directly on the purpose of your life and where you are accomplishing it.

Eating is Sacred. Every time you eat or drink anything, say to yourself, "Eating is sacred. I eat this food to nourish my body."

When you emotionally eat you deprive yourself from learning about your emotions. Next time you go for the cookie when you have had a "bad" day consider sitting down and reflecting on the events of the day and see what you can learn from this.

What is more worthy of your attention—a gift of knowledge about yourself or a cookie?

The Carbohydrate Type Diet

Relatively weak appetite-a little food goes a long way. Sometimes you may eat three meals a day but often the meals will be small. It is still important to eat even if it is a snack. **"Mindfully under eating"**.

Tolerance for sweets- You may be able to tolerate an occasional sweet but watch that you don't grab the sweets whenever you are hungry for energy. This could lead to eventually becoming hypoglycemic, insulin resistant and diabetes.

Weight Management- Because your appetite is small the tendency may be to skip a meal or eat high sugary foods that may lead to weigh gain. Be sure and eat at least three times a day and include protein in your meal or snack.

Type-A Personality- The sympathetic dominants have classic Type A personalities. They tend to be aggressive and goal-oriented. Finding time to eat sometimes does not happen.

Caffeine Dependency- Depending on caffeine to get them through the day; leads to adrenal exhaustion, weakened appetite and a dive in your energy; creating the need for more caffeine!

By emphasizing the proper metabolic type® diet for this type you will be able to have great energy all day without the use of sugar or caffeine.

"Fail to Plan, Plan to Fail"

- **Eat low fat proteins** such as chicken breast or pork.
- **Watch the dairy** and use small amounts and low fat.
- **Balance the carbohydrates** 3 veggies to 1 fruit ratio.
- **Eat grains** only after you have eaten your proteins and vegetables. Do not eat refined white products only whole grains.
- **Vegetable juices** are great for your type if they are freshly made. However they should be mainly "green" juices not carrot as this is too high in sugar. Avoid fruit juices.
- **Limit Legumes-** Watch your intake of beans as they are higher in purines then other carbohydrates. ½-1 cup occasionally especially if you are eating a vegetarian meal.
- **Watch your fats-** This does not mean to not eat fats but use them sparingly. A little bit goes along way.
- **Easy on the nuts-** Nuts are a great source of protein but they are also high in fat. ¼ cup per day of unsalted raw organic nuts is generally just right.
- **Moderation of alcohol, caffeine and sugar-** It is poison to your body. Be responsible and **"Pick your poison"**. Limit the intake or avoid them.

Food Menu's for Carbohydrate Type #1-O

Breakfast

Protein smoothie (see recipes) or
Egg Frittata with fruit or a zucchini muffin or
Almond meal pancakes with fruit or
Yogurt with fruit and nuts or
Hot whole grain cereal with milk and fruit or
One or two eggs poached on a piece of non wheat toast with fruit

Lunch

Italian Vegetable soup or
Lentil Salad or
Bowl White Bean Chili or
Bowl Black Bean Chili or
Tomato stuffed with white tuna salad with a cup of soup or
Chicken Suma salad

Dinner

Turkey meatloaf with Quinoa corn salad or
Chicken breast with Mediterranean couscous or
Baked fish with green salad or
Chicken Enchilada with Black Bean Salad or
Greek Moussaka with Fig Salad

Snacks

½ pc of fruit with ¼ cup nuts or
3 ounces plain low-fat yogurt with ½ cup berries or
1 Tablespoon peanut butter with ½ an apple or
1 ounce Swiss cheese with a pear

Shopping List for 1-O

Green = Ideal (eat these foods at every meal)
Black = For variety (but emphasize "Ideal" foods)
Italics = Caution (eat only rarely)

Proteins
Pork Ham or Tenderloin
Chicken (light meat)
Cornish Hen
Ostrich
Turkey (light meat)
Turkey (dark meat)
Chicken (dark meat)
Beef
Lamb
Pork (bacon, chops, rib)
Duck
Goose
Pheasant
Quail
Wild game
Bass (freshwater & sea)
Cod
Flounder
Grouper
Halibut
Mahi-mahi
Perch
Rockfish
Roughy
Snapper
Tuna (light)
Turbot
Catfish
Pompano
Shark
Snail/Escargot
Swordfish
Whitefish
Abalone
Arctic char
Clam
Crab
Crayfish
Lobster
Octopus
Oyster
Perch(ocean)
Salmon
Shrimp
Trout
Tuna (dark)

Legumes
Black eyed peas
Garbanzo Beans
Navy Beans
Pink Beans
Pinto Beans
White Beans
Adzuki Beans
Black Beans
Fava Beans
Great Northern Beans
Lima Beans
Mung Beans
Red Beans
Tempeh

Dairy and Eggs
Blue Cheese
Brie
Camembert
Cheddar
Colby
Cream
Cream Cheese
Edam
Goat Cheese
Gouda
Gruyere
Milk (whole)
Monterey Jack
Muenster
Parmesan
Provolone
Romano
Roquefort
Swiss
Buttermilk
Cottage Cheese
Cow Milk (whole)
Cream (half & half)
Feta
Goat Cheese
Kefir Mozzarella
Nuefchatel
Ricotta
Sour Cream
Whey Protein
Yogurt (full fat)
Eggs, chicken
Eggs, Duck

Nuts and seeds
Almonds
Cashews
Chestnuts
Pine Nuts
Pistachios
Poppy Seeds
Sesame Seeds
Sunflower Seeds
Brazil Nuts
Filbert/Hazelnuts
Flax
Hickory Nuts
Macadamia Nuts
Peanuts
Pecans
Pumpkin Seeds
Walnuts

Oils and Fats
Butter unsalted
Coconut oil
Ghee
Olive Oil
Palm Kernel Oil
Butter salted
Almond/Walnut Oil
Hemp Oil
Peanut Oil
Sesame Oil
Sunflower Oil

Grains
Cornmeal
Rice (basmati)
Rice (brown)
Spelt
Triticale
Wild Rice
Amaranth
Buckwheat
Kamut
Quinoa
Millet

Vegetables
Arugula
Beet Greens
Cilantro
Dandelion Greens
Endive
Kale
Mustard Greens
Parsley
Radicchio
Sprouts (alfalfa & bean)
Swiss Chard
Broccoli
Brussels Sprouts
Cabbage
Cucumber
Pepper (hot, bell & all colors)
Tomato
Bamboo Shoots
Bok Choy
Daikon
Eggplant
Jicama
Kohlrabi
Radish
Water Chestnuts
Zucchini
Parsnips Pumpkin
Potato (all kinds)
Squash (summer)
Collard Greens
Lettuces (bibb, leaf & romaine)
Turnip Greens
Watercress
Avocado
Celery
Fennel
Garlic
Ginger root
Leeks
Olives (all kinds)
Onion
Okra
Scallion
Shallot
Turnip
Beet
Carrot
Corn
Squash (winter)
Sweet potato
Yam

Fruits
Apricot
Blackberry
Blueberry
Boysenberry
Cherry
Cranberry
Elderberry
Gooseberry
Grape
Loganberry
Kumquat
Nectarine
Papaya
Peach
Pear
Plum
Raspberry
Rhubarb
Strawberry
Banana
Cantaloupe
Casaba Melon
Guava
Honeydew Melon
Kiwifruit
Mango
Papaya
Persimmon
Pineapple
Pomegranate
Watermelon
Apple
Banana
 Coconut
Grapefruit
Lemon
Lime
Orange
Tangerine
Currant(dried)
Prune
Date
Fig (dried)
Raisin

Beverages
Water (filtered
Rice Milk
Tea (Black, Green &Herbal)
Vegetable Juice
Almond Milk
Coffee (decaf)
Coffee
Raw Cow Milk
Raw Goat Milk

Begin the Day
Carbohydrate types feel best when they start the day with fruits and vegetables and a small amount of protein and fat which can be found in dairy.

Almond Pancakes
(Calories per pancake: 125, 6 g protein, 8 g fat, 6 g carbohydrates)

Makes 4-6 pancakes

1	Mix ingredients together and cook as you would other pancakes.	1 C. almond meal 2 eggs ¼ C. water ¼ C. chopped apples 2 T. coconut oil 1 T. stevia or ½ T. maple syrup
	They will not bubble, so turn when side becomes light brown.	½ t. cinnamon ¼ t. sea salt
2	Serve with pat of butter and chopped walnuts and sliced bananas or apples.	butter walnuts banana

Tip: You must use medium high heat to cook through and brown. Keep warm in oven while making others will also make them cook through.

Banana Coconut Flour Nut Muffins

(Calories: 184, 12 g protein, 8 g fat, 16 g carbohydrates)

Makes 12 muffins

1	Preheat oven to 350° F	
2	Mix coconut flour and baking powder in a separate bowl, set aside.	1 C. coconut flour* 1 t. baking powder
3	In a mixing bowl, beat eggs gradually…. Add milk, stevia, coconut oil, butter, vanilla and salt.	6 organic free range eggs 2 T. organic milk 1 T. stevia (substitute 1/3 C. maple syrup) 2 T. coconut oil* (warmed to liquid) 2 T. organic butter ½ t. vanilla 1/8 t. sea salt
4	Mash the bananas and add to the egg mixture. Continue mixing and slowly add the flour mixture and walnuts and mix until blended.	2 green tipped bananas ½ C. walnut pieces
5	Oil and fill muffin cups with batter.	
6	Bake for 20 minutes.	

*Purchase at www.tropicaltraditions.com

Egg white Frittata

(Calories: 280, 24 g protein, 8 g fat 29 g carbohydrates)

1	Preheat oven to 400° F	
2	Oil and sprinkle pie or quiche pan with almond meal and set aside.	1 T olive or coconut oil ¼ C. almond meal(optional)
3	In a skillet melt butter; sauté onions, zucchini and red pepper until light brown, 4-5 minutes. Top with the leaves and cover and simmer 3-4 more minutes.	1-2 T. olive oil or coconut oil 1 onion, chopped 1-2 zucchini, chopped(may use yellow squash) 1 red pepper, chopped 4 oz. spinach or kale leaves, chopped
4	Crumble the feta and sprinkle over the mixture evenly.	4 oz. feta (may use goat)
5	Mix egg whites and milk together in a bowl until light and fluffy Beat in eggs until well mixed.	¼ C. almond , rice milk or organic milk 6 organic egg whites 6 organic egg (may use less eggs and more whites)
6	Place vegetable mixture in pan with almond meal crust.	
7	Pour egg mixture over all and top with Gomasio	1 t. Gomasio (organic sesame seeds and sea salt)
8	Bake for 30 minutes.	Serves Six

Salmon Omelet

(Calories: 250, 24 g protein, 13 g fat, 8 g carbohydrates)

Serves 2

1	Preheat oven to 350° F	
2	Separate egg yolks and lightly beat, set side. Combine the 4 egg whites in a small mixing bowl and beat until light and fluffy. Add salt and pepper to taste and egg yolks.	2 large organic eggs and 2 egg whites ¼ t. sea salt ¼ t. pepper
3	Lightly oil an oven proof skillet and place over medium heat. Spread the egg mixture in the pan and cook for 3-5 minutes until the bottom is light brown.	1 T. coconut oil or butter
4	Place the skillet in the hot oven on the middle rack and bake 3 minutes. Dot with goat cheese, salmon and tomatoes and parsley and bake 1 more minute.	3 oz. goat cheese 3 oz. smoked salmon (or left over salmon)* 4 cherry tomatoes split in half ¼ C. parsley, chopped
5	To serve fold the omelet in half.	

Tip: Serve this with a bowl of fresh fruit and a piece of manna bread.

Zucchini Muffins
(Calories: 180, 3 g protein, 8 g fat, 24 g carbohydrates)

Makes 12 muffins or 24 mini

1	Preheat oven to 375° F	
2	Grate. Set aside.	2 C. zucchini
3	Chop. Set aside.	½ C. walnuts
4	Sift into a bowl…	1½ C. quinoa flour
		1 C. coconut flour
		½ C. protein powder
		1 T. baking soda
		2 t. cinnamon
		1 t. ground ginger
	… and then add the grated zucchini and chopped walnuts.	¼ t. ground cloves
		½ t. sea salt
		½ C. raisins
5	In a coffee grinder or blender, grind flaxseeds. Add the water and mix until blended and slightly gummy.	3 T. flaxseeds, ground
		½ C. water
		½ C. apple juice
		½ C. maple syrup
		1 t. vanilla
	To the flaxseed mixture, add apple juice, maple syrup, oil and vanilla and mix until foamy.	1/3 C. coconut oil (warmed to liquid)
6	Pour wet mixture into dry mixture and mix well (You may need a little extra apple juice).	
7	Spoon into oiled muffin tins	
8	Bake for 20-25 minutes	

Nancy's No-Carb Zucchini Muffins
(Calories: 170, 7 g protein, 14 g fat, 2 g carbohydrates)

Makes 18 small muffins

1	Preheat oven to 350° F	
2	Grate. Set aside.	3 C. zucchini
3	Chop. Set aside.	1 C. walnuts
4	Sift into a bowl… … and then add the grated zucchini and chopped walnuts.	2 C. almond meal ½ C. whey protein powder 1 t. baking soda 2 t. cinnamon 1 t. ground ginger 1 t. ground nutmeg ¼ t. ground cloves ¼ t. sea salt
5	Mix together in another bowl.	3 organic free range eggs, slightly whipped ¼ C. maple syrup 1 t. vanilla 1/3 C. coconut oil ¼ C. apple juice
6	Pour wet mixture into dry mixture and mix well (You may need a little extra apple juice to make a soft batter).	
7	Spoon into a small muffin tin.	
8	Bake for 20-25 minutes.	

Protein Smoothies

Serves one each recipe: In blender

1	Basic berry-Combine milk, with frozen fruit and scoop of protein powder in blender. May add ground nuts or LSA* if desired for extra fiber.	1-1½ C. organic rice or almond milk ½ C. frozen fruit *1 scoop whey, hemp, egg white or rice protein powder 1-2 T. almond or peanut butter
2	**Creamy monkey**-Mix milk, protein powder, peanut or almond butter, banana and blend.	1-1½ C. organic rice or almond milk *1 scoop whey, hemp, egg white or rice protein powder 1 T. peanut or almond butter ½ frozen banana
3	**Reese's pieces**-Same ingredients as creamy monkey but add organic cocoa powder.	Use 1 T. cocoa powder to above recipe for Creamy monkey.
4	**Tropical delight**-Combine milk with coconut milk, mango, almond butter, protein powder and blend until smooth.	1 C. organic rice or almond milk ½ C. coconut milk 1 C. frozen organic mangos *1 scoop whey, egg white, hemp or rice protein powder 1-2 T. almond butter
5	**Raspberry delight**-Blend milk, protein powder, raspberries, almond butter and cocoa until smooth.	1-1½ C. organic milk, rice or almond milk *1 scoop whey, hemp, egg white or rice protein powder ½ C. frozen raspberries 1 T. cocoa (optional) 1-2 T. almond butter
6	**Ginger peach**- Blend Milk, peaches, ginger and almond butter together until smooth	1½ C organic rice or almond milk *1 scoop whey, hemp, egg white or rice protein powder 1 C. frozen peaches 1 t. sliced fresh ginger 1 T. almond butter.

* Whey, hemp, egg white or rice are all different types of protein powders. Select one that does not have added sugars. Add the correct amount according to directions on the container to make a smoothie with approximately 18-24 grams of protein.

Salads and more
60% of your diet should come from carbohydrates.
Eat one or two salads a day.

Pear and Walnut Green Salad
(Calories: 200, 3 g protein, 8 g fat, 16 g carbohydrates)

Serves 4

1	Blend together ….. until emulsified.	4 T. walnut oil (may use olive oil) 4 T. balsamic vinegar ¼ t. sea salt ¼ t. pepper
2	Wash and combine greens in a large bowl and toss the crumbled gorgonzola cheese on the greens.	12 oz. organic greens 2 oz. gorgonzola cheese
3	Thinly slice the pear, skin and all. Slice the onion and add pear and onion to the greens.	1 organic pear ¼ red onion
4	Toast the walnuts and add to salad.	¼ C. walnuts
5	Drizzle the vinaigrette over salad and serve.	

Tip: Adding cooked chicken breast to this salad will make this a complete meal for your type. Enjoy!

Fresh Fig Salad with Toasted Walnuts
(Calories: 280, 8 g protein, 16 g fat, 24 g carbohydrates)

Makes 6 small servings

1	Clean and wipe the figs gently and cut in half. Wash the greens. Arrange 4-5 figs on each plate on top of the greens.	24 fresh black figs, medium size (can use dried) 4 oz. organic baby green lettuce mix
2	Crumble and sprinkle the feta cheese over the figs. Toast and chop the walnuts and scatter on top.	6 oz. feta goat cheese ½ C. walnut halves
3	Place vinegar and salt and pepper in a screw top jar and shake until salt dissolves. Add mustard and walnut oil; shake until emulsified.	1 T. white balsamic vinegar ¼ t. sea salt ¼ t. pepper 1 t. Dijon mustard 6 T. walnut oil
4	Drizzle vinaigrette over fig salad and serve.	

Tip: This makes a light lunch.

Chicken Suma Salad

(1 cup serving: calories 280, 24 g protein, 8 g fat, 28 g carbohydrates)

Serves 6-8

1	Shred the cabbage; chop the green onions and add together in a medium bowl.	1 head of cabbage 8 green onions
2	Add the almonds and the sesame to the cabbage.	¼ C. slivered almonds ¼ C. sesame seeds
3	In a small bowl combine the oils, vinegar and honey with the salt and pepper and add ½ the package of seasoning from the ramen mix.	1/3 C. olive oil 1 T. sesame oil 6 T. rice vinegar 2 T. honey (may use maple syrup) ¼ t. sea salt ¼ t. pepper 2 3 oz. packages ramen style noodles (baked)
4	Add cold chicken to cabbage mixture.	2-3 chicken breasts or thighs, boneless, skinless cooked and cubed
5	Right before serving crush the noodles and add them to the salad.	
6	Toss in the salad dressing and serve.	

Quinoa Corn Salad

(1 cup serving: Calories: 235, 10 g protein, 4 g fat, 40 g carbohydrates)

Serves 4

1	Bring the water or broth to a light boil in a medium saucepan.	1 C. quinoa 2 C. water or vegetable broth
	Rinse the quinoa in cold water before placing in the saucepan with the cooking water or broth. Simmer twenty minutes. If there is extra liquid drain quinoa and place in a bowl.	
2	Combine corn, scallions and cilantro with quinoa and chill.	½ C. frozen corn 2 scallions, chopped 1 T. cilantro leaves
3	Divide greens and place on four salad plates.	14 oz. package of baby greens, rinsed
4	Combine olive oil. Salt and pepper and lime juice and shake until emulsified. Pour over quinoa mixture, and stir together.	1-2 T. olive oil ¼ t. sea salt ¼ t. pepper juice of one organic lime
5	Divide quinoa and place over each bed of lettuce. Sprinkle pumpkins seeds over and serve.	2 T. pumpkin seed,

Black Bean, Corn and Red Pepper Salad

(Calories: 145, 6 g protein, 5 g fat, 19 g carbohydrates)

Serves 4-6

1	Defrost the corn and place in a bowl. Drain the black beans and add to the bowl.	2 C. organic frozen corn 2 C. organic black beans (1 can 14.5 ounces)
2	Dice the red pepper and onion and add to the bowl.	1 large red pepper ½ red onion
3	Chop the cilantro using the leaves only. Add to the bowl.	½ C. cilantro
4	In a small bowl whisk together olive oil, lime juice and salt and pepper.	¼ C. olive oil juice of one lime ¼ t. sea salt ¼ t. pepper
5	Pour olive oil mixture over corn and beans and toss.	
6	Serve at room temperature or chill.	
7	May be refrigerated for 4 days.	

Tip: Serve with Chicken Enchiladas.

Ceviche Recipe Mexican Appetizer

(Serving ½ Cup: Calories: 120, 20 g protein, 2 g fat, 6 g carbohydrates)

Serves 6-8

1	Use only very fresh fish or frozen wild caught.	
2	Defrost, clean and dry fish, remove skin and bones. Dice fish into ¼ inch pieces and place in a casserole dish. Cover with lime juice and refrigerate for 2 hours.	¼ lb. each, white fish, halibut, shrimp, tuna 2 C. lime juice
3	Stir, refrigerate 2 more hours. Drain off lime juice.	
4	Mince jalapeño pepper, onion and garlic and place in a separate bowl along with chopped tomatoes and chopped cilantro.	2 jalapeño peppers 1 medium onion 1-2 cloves fresh garlic 1 C. tomatoes, chopped 1/3 C. cilantro leaves, chopped
5	Whisk together in another bowl and add to tomato mixture. Stir into fish, coating completely. Refrigerate 3 more hours…	3 T. olive oil 2 T. apple cider vinegar ¼ t. oregano, dried ½ t. sea salt ½ t. pepper
6	Bring to room temperature (about 15 minutes) and serve on a bed of lettuce with avocado slices.	Bibb lettuce 1-2 Avocado

Arugula or Kale Salad
(Calories: 260, 12 g protein, 13 g fat, 26 g carbohydrates)

Serves 2 full meal or 4 small

1	Place eggs in saucepan and add enough water to cover them. Bring to low boil and then reduce heat to medium low for 10 minutes. Pour off the hot water and run under cold water to cool them. Once cooled peel the eggs and chop them.	4 free-range eggs 1 qt. water
2	Mix ingredients together. …set aside	3 T. walnut oil (may use olive oil) 1 T. goat chevre cheese, crumbled ¼ t. season salt ¼ t. pepper
3	Toss the leaves with ½ the dressing and place on the salad plates. Top with chopped eggs, beets, carrots and pine nuts. Drizzle with the remaining 2 Tablespoons dressing.	6 C. arugula or kale leaves, cleaned and dried 2 fresh beets steamed and sliced or 1 8 oz. can of beets, rinsed and sliced 1 C. carrots, shredded 2 T. pine nuts, toasted

Tip: To toast nuts or seeds: Cook in a small dry skillet over medium–low heat, stirring constantly, until fragrant and lightly browned about 2-4 minutes.

Lentil Salad

(1/2 C. serving 200 calories, 12 g protein, 4 g fat, 29 g carbohydrates)

Serves 4

1	Sort through and wash the lentils. In a pot cover the lentils with water. Bring to a boil, add bay leaf, cover and lower heat to a simmer, stirring occasionally and cook for 20-25 minutes until done. Drain in a colander.	1½ C. lentils 1 bay leaf
2	Soak currants in hot water for approximately 15 minutes, drain.	¼ C. currants ½ C. water
3	In a medium pan sauté onion in oil until soft about 5 minutes. Chop carrot and add to onion in pan for 2 minutes.	2 T. olive oil ½ C. onion 1 medium carrot
4	Place drained lentils in with the onion mixture and toss in the pine nuts and soy sauce.	¼ C. pine nuts 1 T. tamari wheat free soy sauce
5	Serve warm or at room temperature.	

Hummus

(2 tablespoons Calories 60, 2 g protein, 2 g fat, 8 g carbohydrates)

Makes 1 ½ cups

1 Using a food processor combine chickpeas (garbanzos), tahini, lemon juice, garlic, cumin, salt and olive oil. Blend until smooth.

2 With motor still running, slowly add chick pea liquid until desired consistency is reached.

3 Place hummus in bowl and sprinkle with paprika.

2 C. chickpeas (save liquid)
4 T. organic tahini
3 T. lemon juice
1 clove garlic, minced
1 t. ground cumin
1 t. sea salt
2 T. olive oil
½ to ¼ C. chickpea liquid

paprika

Tip: This makes a great dip or snack served with raw vegetables.

Papaya Salsa

(Calories: 80 per ¼ cup, 0 g protein, 0 g fat, 20 g carbohydrates)

Makes one cup

1	Blend together.	1½ C. papaya, cubed and peeled 2 T. lime juice 1 T. water
2	Stir in.	¼ C. cilantro, chopped 2 t. jalapeño, minced ¼ t. sea salt ¼ t. pepper
3	May be refrigerated up to 1 week.	

Tip: Great served with Grilled Chicken or Shrimp.

Soups and one pot meals

This is a great way to get added vegetables in our meals. Be sure and add protein to the meal if the recipe does not call for it.

Vegetable Broth #1

Makes 1 ½ quart

1	Cut up vegetables into ½ inch pieces and place them in a soup pan with 1 quart of filtered water or vegetable broth. Bring to a boil and then simmer for 6-8 minutes.	1 qt. vegetable broth or filtered water 2-3 zucchini ½ bunch parsley 2-3 celery stalks 1 C. broccoli 1 small potato
2	Puree in a blender and add lemon, olive oil tamari and salt and pepper to taste.	juice of ½ lemon 1 T. olive oil 1 T. tamari wheat free soy sauce or Bragg's Aminos ¼ t. sea salt ¼ t. pepper
3	May be refrigerated for 2-3 days.	

Tip: This is a great way to get more vegetables in. Drink anytime hot or cold.

Chicken Bone Broth

Makes 1-2 pints

1 pastured organic chicken, bones only
2 qt. filtered water
2 T. apple cider vinegar

1. Place bones in a large pot and cover with water and add the vinegar. Let stand for one hour.

2. Bring the pot to a simmering low boil and remove any foam scum that appears on the top of the water. Continue simmering on low boil for 24 hours.

3. Remove bones and place in a container. Use or freeze for later use.

Cleansing Broth

(Calories per cup 70, 2 g protein, 3 g fat, 9 g carbohydrates)

1	Steam or boil the sweet potato for 10 minutes.	1 medium sweet potato, peeled and quartered
2	In a 4 quart pan add water, squash, zucchini, cabbage, spinach and celery and cook for 8 minutes.	1 qt. filtered water 1-2 yellow squash or zucchini 3-4 oz. cabbage, chopped 4 oz. spinach or kale leaves 3-4 stalks celery, chopped
3	Add sweet potatoes to the pan.	
4	Puree in blender adding the olive oil, tamari and milk and gelatin.	1-2 T. olive oil 1-2 T. tamari wheat free soy sauce 1 C. rice milk or unsweetened almond milk 2-3 T. *great Lakes gelatin (porcine) optional
5	Serve immediately. May be refrigerated and reheated or enjoyed at room temperature or chilled.	
6	Last in refrigerator 2-3 days.	

Tip: This broth can be made and drank in-between meals for added carbohydrates or used as a de-tox cleanse. If using for a cleanse omit the gelatin. * Great Lakes gelatin can be purchased at www.greatlakesgelatin.com porcine formula or bovine.

Butternut Soup

(Calories: 150, 3 g protein, 2 g fat, 33 g carbohydrates)

Serves 4-6

1	Cut the butternut squash in half and remove the seeds and cut into large chunks. Steam or bake at 350° for ½ hour or until flesh is tender.	2½ lb. butternut squash
2	Let squash cool and remove the skin and put into blender or food processor with water. Blend until smooth.	1 C. filtered water
3	Sauté onion in oil until soft about 3-5 minutes and add to the blender with the squash.	½ T. olive oil ½ C. onion, diced
4	Add spices, tamari sauce and coconut milk to mixture and blend.	¼ t. cayenne ¼ t. curry powder ½ T. tamari wheat free soy sauce 1 C. coconut milk
5	Heat and serve.	

Tip: You need to add some protein like Orange-Ginger Chicken for a complete meal.

Lentil Vegetable Soup

((Calories: 230, 17 g protein, 7 g fat, 25 g carbohydrates)

Serves 6-8

1	Heat oil in a large Dutch oven or stockpot over medium heat. Add onions, celery, carrots and bay leaves; sauté for 10 minutes.	1 T. olive oil 1 1/3 C. onions, chopped fine 1/3 C. celery, diced 1/3 C. carrots, diced 2 bay leaves
2	To the pot add tomato paste, salt and garlic and sauté another minute.	2 T. tomato paste 1 t. sea salt 2 garlic cloves, minced
3	Add the water and lentils; bring to a boil, partially cover and reduce heat, simmering for 25 minutes.	6 C. filtered water 1 C. dried dark green lentils (French)
4	Stir in the chopped kale, parsley, vinegar, mustard and pepper and cook on medium for 15 minutes.	6 C. kale or spinach 1/3 C. chopped parsley 2 t. balsamic vinegar 2 t. Dijon mustard ¼ t. black pepper 3 oz. parmesan cheese, grated
5	Discard the bay leaves. Ladle soup into bowls and top with cheese if desired.	

Tip: Serve a salad like Fresh Fig Salad or a big green salad.

Black Bean Soup

(Calories: 210, 4 g protein, 5 g fat, 40 g carbohydrates)

Serves 4-6

1	Prepare the beans (see Black Bean Chili Recipe). If using can, bring beans to a simmer in a medium pot.	2 C. black beans, dried or 1 large can 3½ C. water or chicken broth
2	Add the bay leaf, garlic, onion, green pepper and oregano to the beans and simmer 20 minutes.	1 bay leaf 1-2 cloves of garlic, minced 1 onion, chopped 1 green pepper, chopped 1 t. oregano, dried
3	Remove the bay leaf. Puree half the bean mixture in a blender; then stir them back into the pot and add the vinegar.	2 T. apple cider vinegar
4	Cook for a few minutes longer. If soup is too thick add broth or water. Top with Cilantro cream (recipe below). This soup may be frozen.	
5	To make Cilantro cream blend until smooth.	1 C. plain yogurt 3 T. cilantro, chopped 2 T. lime juice 2 scallions, chopped 1 clove garlic, chopped ¼ t. sea salt pinch of cayenne pepper

Black Bean Chili

(Calories: 350, 18 g protein, 4 g fat, 28 g carbohydrates)

Serves 8-12 1 cup size

1	Pick over the beans and discard any broken beans or rocks. Soak over night in enough filtered water to cover by 2 inches.	3 C. dried black beans (may use 3 cans)
2	Drain the beans and place in a large soup pot and add water to cover beans, approximately 1 quart. Bring to a boil, reduce heat, cover and simmer on high for one hour. Add water if necessary.	1 qt. filtered water
3	In a pan heat oil and sauté onions, bell pepper, celery, carrots and garlic until light brown about 8 minutes.	2 t. olive oil 1 large onion, chopped 1 red bell pepper, chopped 2-3 stalks celery, chopped 2-3 carrots, chopped 2-3 cloves garlic. minced
4	Deglaze the pan using tequila or lime juice scraping up any brown bits.	1 T. tequila (may use lime juice)
5	Stir in spices and chipotle peppers with adobo sauce. Add ground meat and tomato paste and cook until meat is brown about 5 minutes	1 t. oregano, dried ½ t. cumin ½ t. coriander 2 chipotle peppers seeded and chopped in adobo sauce 1 T. tomato paste 1 lb. ground turkey
6	Drain the beans and add the onion mixture to the bean pot. Add broth and bring to a boil, lower, cover and simmer for 1 hour.	1-2 C. chicken broth

7	Add sea salt, lime juice and cilantro just before serving.	½ T. sea salt 1 lime 1-2 T. cilantro, chopped
8	May freeze for up to 3 months.	

Tip: This tastes even better the next day. Be sure and serve with a fresh green salad or other vegetables.

White Bean Chili
(Calories: 230, 12 g protein, 4 g fat, 37 g carbohydrates)

Serves 6-8

1	Soak beans overnight in enough water to cover by 2 inches. Drain and place in a 4-quart pot.	2 C. dried northern white, soaked, (may use white beans)
2	Add water and bay leaves to beans and bring to a boil; reduce heat and simmer 40 minutes.	6 C. filtered water 2 bay leaves
3	Heat oil in a skillet; add onion and garlic and sauté briefly.	2 T. olive oil 2 medium onions, chopped fine 3 cloves garlic, minced
4	Add the paprika, chili powder and cumin to the onion mixture and sauté 2 minutes.	1 T. sweet paprika 1-2 T. chili powder 1 t. cumin
5	Add the tomatoes and ground meat and cook until browned.	1 large can diced tomatoes 1 lb. ground turkey or beef
6	Remove the bay leaves and all but 2 cups of the bean liquid from the beans. Add the onion mixture and simmer for 1 hour or until the beans are soft.	

Chicken and Spinach Soup with Fresh Pesto

(1 ½ cup serving: 204, 18 g protein, 8 g fat, 16 g carbohydrates)

Serves 6-8

1	Heat the oil in a large Dutch oven over medium heat. Add the carrots and the chicken; cook turning the chicken and stirring frequently about 3-4 minutes.	1 T. olive oil ½ organic carrot, chopped 6-8 chicken thighs, boned and skinned
2	Add broth and marjoram bring to a boil and then reduce to a simmer for 5 minutes.	5 C. chicken broth 1½ t. marjoram, dried
3	With a slotted spoon take the chicken pieces out and place on a cutting board.	
4	Add leaves and beans to the soup and bring to a low boil for 5 minutes.	6 oz. spinach leaves 1 15-oz. can great northern beans, rinsed
5	In a food processor combine oil, cheese, basil and nuts. Process until course paste forms adding water if necessary.	2 T. olive oil ¼ C. goat cheddar cheese, grated ¼ C. basil leaves, fresh 2 T. pine nuts
6	Cut the chicken into bite size pieces and stir into soup along with the pesto made from the food processor.	
7	Season with pepper. Heat until hot.	¼ t. pepper

Tip: This is a wonderful soup that can be a light meal or the first course for a heartier meal.

Italian Vegetable Soup with Chicken
(Calories: 250, 24 g protein, 4 g fat, 28 g carbohydrates)

Makes a big pot, can be frozen

1	In a six quart pot; heat oil and cook onion, celery and carrots until soft about 5 minutes. Add water and broth, whole chicken; cover and simmer one hour. Remove the chicken and de-bone and skin and return to pot.	2 T. olive oil 3 C. onion, chopped 2 C. celery, chopped 1 C. carrots, chopped 2 qts. chicken broth 1-2 qt. filtered water 1 whole organic chicken
2	Add bay leaves, tomatoes, thyme, basil, oregano and garlic to the pot; cover and simmer 20 minutes.	3 bay leaves 8 C. tomatoes(two large cans) 1 T. thyme 1 2 T. basil, dried 1 T. oregano, dried 4 cloves garlic, minced
3	Add parsley, broccoli, cauliflower, zucchini, kidney beans, garbanzo beans and leaves simmering for 5-6 minutes.	½ C. parsley leaves, chopped 2 C. each broccoli, cauliflower, zucchini, chopped 1 C. kidney beans (medium can) 1 C. garbanzo beans (medium can) 2 C. spinach or kale leaves
4	Add vinegar and tamari (soy sauce) and simmer 2-3 minutes.	1 t. cider vinegar 1 T. tamari wheat free soy sauce
5	Remove bay leaves and add sea salt and pepper. Remove from heat and garnish with cheese.	1 t. sea salt ½ t. pepper parmesan cheese for topping (optional)

Creamy Potato and Greens Soup

(Calories: 200, 4 g protein, 4 g fat, 40 g carbohydrates)

Serves 4-6

1	In a 4 quart pot, sauté in oil the onions, leeks and cook until tender about 8 minutes.	1 T. olive oil 1 C. onion, chopped 2-3 leeks, chopped white part only
2	Add broth and bring to a boil.	4 C. vegetable broth
3	Add potatoes, fennel, celery, vinegar and dill and simmer on medium heat for 20 minutes, covered.	4 C. organic potatoes, chopped ¼ t. fennel ground ½ C. celery, chopped 1 T. apple cider vinegar ½ t. dill, dried
4	Puree in blender or use immersion blender. Return to pot and add mustard, scallions, basil and milk. Stir until mixed.	2 t. Dijon mustard 2 T. minced scallions 1½ T. fresh basil, minced ½ C. organic whole milk
5	In a separate pot gently steam or boil the greens for 6-8 minutes. Strain and add to soup with salt and pepper and lemon juice to taste.	4 C. loosely packed greens such as kale or chard, shredded ¼ t. sea salt ¼ t. pepper 1 T. lemon juice
6	Serve warm in individual bowls. May be refrigerated 3-4 days.	

Potato Leek Soup

(Calories per cup: 175, 2 g protein, 4 g fat, 30 g carbohydrates)

Serves 4-6

1	Carefully wash and chop leeks and place in a 2 quart pot with oil and butter and cook until soft.	2-3 leeks 1 T. olive oil 1 T. butter
2	Chop potatoes and onions and add to the pot along with the chicken broth. Lower the heat and simmer 30 minutes.	2-3 organic potatoes 1 medium onion 2 qts. chicken broth
3	Put in a blender or use immersion blender in pot and blend until smooth.	
4	Return to pot and season with sea salt and pepper and lemon juice and heat until just warm enough.	¼ t. sea salt ¼ t. pepper ½ T. lemon juice
5	Serve in individual bowls topped with chopped chives.	1 T. chives, chopped
6	May be refrigerated up to 4 days.	

Tip: This with a big green salad with an added hard boiled egg would make a perfect lunch or light dinner.

Nancy's Cioppino
(Calories: 400, 25 g protein, 8 g fat, 32 g carbohydrates)

Serves 6-8

1. In a large soup pan sauté the onions, green pepper, garlic and fennel in oil until soft about 7 minutes.

2. Add tomatoes, clam juice and pepper and bring to a low boil for about 10 minutes until slightly thickened.

3. Add the fish and lower the heat to medium cook until just done about 2-5 minutes.

4. Ladle into bowls and serve topped with cheese.

2 T. olive oil
1½ onion, chopped
1 green bell pepper, diced
2-3 cloves garlic, minced
1-2 fennel bulbs, diced
1 large or 2 medium cans tomatoes, diced
2 bottles clam juice
¼ t. black pepper

½ lb. each, halibut, bass, tuna and shrimp, cleaned and deveined

1 T. each parmesan cheese grated

Tip: This served with the Pear Walnut Salad makes a great meal.

Roasted Pumpkin Soup

(1 Cup Calories: 130, 3 g protein, 6 g fat, 19g carbohydrates)

Serves 6

1	Preheat oven to 375° F	
2	Cut pumpkin into quarters or large chunks. Remove seeds and pithy pulp.	2 lb. pumpkins (small baking type)
3	Place pumpkin and onion halves, cut side down on an oiled baking sheet. Place the white part of the leeks and the garlic unpeeled on the baking sheet along with the pumpkin.	1 large onion, halved 3 leeks, white part only, cut in half 3 cloves garlic 1 T. olive oil
4	Brush vegetables with olive oil, cover with foil and bake for 25 minutes. … Peel vegetables, including garlic then coarsely chop and place in a bowl.	2 T. olive oil
5	In a 4-5 quart saucepan heat oil with butter. Add ginger and apple and sauté until softened.	1 T. olive oil 1 T. butter 2 t. ginger root, minced 1 apple, peeled, cored and diced
6	Sir into the saucepan the curry powder, the baked vegetables and the chicken broth. Bring to a boil, cover and lower the heat to simmer for 15 minutes.	1 t. curry powder 3 C. chicken broth

7	Puree the mixture in batches or use an immersion blender and blend until smooth. Add lemon or lime juice.	2 T. lemon or lime juice
8	Return the soup to the pot, stir in milk and heat through just to warm. Pour into bowls and garnish with chopped chives and gorgonzola cheese.	1 C. organic whole milk 3 T. chives, chopped ½ C. gorgonzola cheese, crumbled

Fennel and Lemon Soup

(Calories: 95, 4 g protein, 5 g fat, 10 g carbohydrates)

Serves 4-6

1	In a 2 Quart pot heat oil and add onions and cook 5 minutes.	1 T. olive oil 1 onion, chopped
2	Add fennel pieces and cook 5 more minutes.	2 fennel bulbs, thinly chopped
3	Add broth and lemon zest and bring to a boil; reduce heat, cover and simmer for 20 minutes.	2½ C. chicken broth 1 organic lemon, zest
4	Transfer to blender and process until smooth. Add milk to give the desired consistency and season with salt and pepper.	1 C. coconut milk ¼ t. sea salt ¼ t. pepper
5	Stir in the lemon juice just before serving and garnish with fennel leaves and a wedge of lemon.	juice of one organic lemon fennel leaves
6	May be served hot or cold.	

Tip: This served with Grilled Chicken with Papaya Salsa completes the meal.

Chilled Cantaloupe and Mint Soup
(Calories: 104, 4 g protein, 1 g fat, 15 g carbohydrates)

Serves 4

1	Peel the cantaloupe and place in blender with mint leaves. Blend until smooth	1 medium cantaloupe 1½ T. mint leaves
2	Add yogurt and wine and blend for 30 seconds.	1 C. organic plain yogurt ½ C. white wine (may use mineral water)
3	Chill over night pour into small bowls or parfait glasses and serve with a sprig of mint.	

Tip: This is a great summer soup served with Bacon Wrapped Pork Tenderloin and a green salad.

Vegetables and more
60% of your diet should come from carbohydrates

Twice Baked Potatoes

(Calories: 280, 7 g protein, 14 g fat, 25 g carbohydrates)

Serves 4

1	Preheat oven to 425° F	
2	Wash and dry potatoes; rub with olive oil and pierce each one. Place in oven for one hour.	4 medium russet potatoes 1 T. olive oil
3	Cut the top off the potato and scoop out ½ the inside and place in a bowl. Discard the other half.	
4	In the bowl add yogurt, butter, salt and pepper, whipping the mixture until all the lumps are out. Add the green onions and vegetables mixing well.	¼ C. plain yogurt or sour cream 1 T. butter ¼ t. sea salt ¼ t. pepper 2-4 green onions, diced ½ C. broccoli, chopped ½ C. red pepper, diced ¼ C. mozzarella cheese, grated
5	Put mixture back into the potato skins. Sprinkle with cheese. Bake at 350° F for 15 minutes. Serve immediately.	

Tip: To make this a complete meal you might cook 3-4 chicken breasts; chop them and add to the vegetable mixture before baking.

Grilled Vegetable Pie with Brown Rice Crust

(Calories: 300, 10 g protein, 4 g fat, 55 g carbohydrates)

Serves 6-8

1. Preheat oven to 450° F

2. To make crust: Sauté onion and garlic in water or broth and soy sauce for 2 minutes until moisture evaporates.

    1 small onion, chopped
    1 clove garlic, minced
    1 t. tamari wheat free soy sauce
    1/3 C. water or vegetable broth
    1 C. cooked brown rice
    1 C. almond meal

3. Put rice, almond meal and onion mixture in a food processor and blend until sticks together. Using wet fingers, pat mixture into a pie dish forming a crust. Bake for 15 minutes. Set a side.

4. To make filling marinade the vegetables in a dressing for at least 4 hours or over night.

    2-3 zucchini, sliced
    2-3 yellow squash, sliced
    1 eggplant, peeled and sliced
    3-4 tomatoes, sliced
    1-2 onions, sliced
    ¼ C. Italian salad dressing

5. Grill or sauté the vegetables turning as they brown, approximately 10 minutes.

6. Begin layering the vegetables into the crust adding a layer of cheese in between and on top.

    4 oz. cheese, mozzarella or feta
    2 T. parmesan

7. Bake 15 minutes at 325° F.

Mediterranean Vegetable Quinoa

(Calories: 220, 4 g protein, 3 g fat, 47 g carbohydrates)

Serves 6-8

1	Heat oil in large skillet. Add onion, garlic and cook until brown about 5 minutes.	1 T. olive oil 1 onion, chopped 2-3 cloves garlic, minced
2	Add vegetables and spices… … cook for 5- 8 minutes.	1 fennel bulb, chopped 1 red pepper, thinly sliced 1 carrot, chopped 2 zucchini, chopped 1½ C. tomatoes, chopped ¼ C. oil-cured olives, chopped 1 ½ t. basil, dried 1 ½ t. oregano, dried 1 t. sea salt ¼ t. cinnamon
3	Rinse and pour quinoa into boiling water, lower heat and simmer 20 minutes.	1 C. quinoa 2 C. water
4	Drain any liquid from the quinoa and add to vegetables and stir in lemon juice cooking for 5 more minutes.	1-3 T. lemon juice ¼ C. fresh parsley or basil

Add fresh herbs and serve.
May be refrigerated 4 days.

Tip: Add cooked pork or chicken to this recipe and it becomes a complete meal.

Baked Stuffed Onion
(Calories: 110, 2 g protein, 5 g fat, 12 g carbohydrates)

Serves 4-6

1	Preheat oven to 350° F	
2	Slice about 1 inch off each onion. With a melon scooper or spoon hollow out the onions creating a bowl. Slice off enough of the onion to stand upright.	4-6 medium onions. peeled
3	Place onions in a baking dish and pour water or broth around them; bake 30 minutes. While the onions are cooking; in a medium bowl combine the walnuts, almond meal or bread crumbs, salt and pepper, mustard and vinegar until well mixed.	½ C. walnuts, chopped ½ C. almond meal or bread crumbs ½ t. sea salt ¼ t. pepper 2 T. Dijon mustard 1 T. balsamic vinegar 1/3 C. water or vegetable broth
4	Remove onions from the oven; Spoon filling into the onions and bake for 30 minutes. Garnish with parsley and serve immediately.	¼ C. parsley leaves, chopped

Tip: This is a great side dish to be served with Meatloaf or grilled fish and a salad or bowl of soup.

Ratatouille (Vegetable stew)

(Calories: 240, 5 g protein, 4.5 g fat, 48 g carbohydrates)

Serves 6-8

1	In a large skillet sauté onions with garlic until tender, about 5 minutes.	½ T. olive oil 2 onions, sliced 2-3 cloves garlic, minced
2	Add vegetables and herbs; Sauté over medium heat 15 minutes.	1 lb. tomatoes, dice (may use 16 oz. can diced) 1 green or yellow pepper, chopped 1 red pepper, roasted and chopped 1 fennel bulb, chopped 2 small eggplants, peeled and diced 2 zucchini, sliced into ½ inch rounds 1 bay leaf 1 t. each, basil, oregano, thyme placed in cheese cloth and tied with string.
3	Meanwhile fry the bacon; crumble and add to vegetables with salt and pepper.	2 slices bacon ¼ t. sea salt ¼ t. pepper
4	Cover and simmer 15 minutes more over medium low heat. Uncover and cook 10 more minutes. Remove herbs in cheesecloth and bay leaf. Serve at once or refrigerate up to 4 days.	

Tip: Make this into a one pot meal by adding 2 chicken or turkey sausages to number 4.

Protein
25% of your diet should come from protein

Nancy's Spiced Greens and Sausage

(Calories: 280, 20 g protein, 8 g fat, 40 g carbohydrates)

Serves 4

1	Cook sausage in oil in a large skillet over medium heat for about 4 minutes each side or until light brown. Remove from skillet and keep warm	1 T. olive oil 6 turkey, chicken or pork sausages
2	Add onion and apple to the skillet and sauté for 5 minutes.	4 C. onions, sliced 1 C. apple, diced
3	Add fennel, coriander, thyme and garlic and cook for 2 minutes.	1 t. fennel seeds, crushed 1 t. coriander, ground 1 t. thyme, dried 3 cloves garlic, minced
4	Wash and remove stems from greens and chop coarsely. Add to skillet with onions and cook 10 minutes or until greens are soft.	2½ lb. kale, chard or collard greens
5	Add chicken broth and mustard, cover and cook 5 minutes.	½ C. chicken broth 1/8 C. wholegrain mustard seeds
6	Add thyme and sausage and warm through.	1 t. fresh or ¼ dried thyme
7	Drizzle with balsamic vinegar and ground pepper.	1-2 T. balsamic vinegar ¼ t. black pepper

Orange-Ginger Chicken
(Calories: 245, 27 g protein, 4 g fat, 25 g carbohydrates)

Serves 4

1. Heat oil in a large skillet over medium heat. Add chicken and sauté for 5-6 minutes each side.

2. Add marmalade and other ingredients and cook for 2 minutes or until bubbly.

3. Serve immediately.

4 chicken breast, boned and skinned (may use thighs)
1 ½ t. dark sesame oil
½ t. chili oil
½- ¼ C. orange marmalade
3 T. soy sauce
1 T. ginger, minced
1 T. water
2 cloves garlic, minced

Tip: This served with a big green salad and Butternut Soup makes a great meal.

Grilled Chicken with Papaya Salsa

(Calories: 245, 29 g protein, 4 g fat, 23 g carbohydrates)

Serves 4

1	Drizzle lime juice over chicken and potatoes and salt and pepper.	1 T. lime juice 4 chicken breast, boned and skinned (may use thighs) 4 red potatoes, sliced ¼ inch thick ¼ t. sea salt ¼ t. pepper
2	Grill chicken and potatoes over medium flame for about 10 minutes or well done.	

Tip: Serve with Papaya Salsa (see under Salads and more) and a big green salad.

Slow/Low Heat Cooking Techniques

1	Preheat oven to 225° F	Bake 5 minutes per ounce of food
2	Using a glass roasting dish with lid, place chicken skin side up on the bottom. Place lid on securely; Bake for 1 hour and 20 minutes.	1 pound Chicken thighs, breasts or legs with skin and bones
3	Combine ingredients and make into four patties; place in a glass dish. And put lid on; bake 1 hour and 20 minutes.	1 pound of ground beef, turkey or bison ¼- ½ t. herbs (your choice) ¼ t. sea salt ¼ t. pepper
4	Place in a glass dish, drizzle with butter or olive oil, salt and pepper and bake covered for 1 hour and 20 minutes.	1 pound of any firm fish (salmon, halibut, cod bass) 1 T. olive oil or butter ¼ t. sea salt ¼ t. pepper

Tip: Use this technique for vegetables as well. Place squash (whole) pierce the skin and bake 5 minutes per ounce in a glass dish with lid on.

Chicken Curry

(Calories 360, 24 g protein, 14 g fat, 35 g carbohydrates)

Serves 4-6

1	Sauté onions in ghee or butter.	3 T. ghee or unsalted butter 1 onion, chopped
2	Add spices and stir for 3 minutes.	1 T. fenugreek seeds, ground ¼ t. cayenne pepper 1 t. coriander, ground 2 T. turmeric 1 t. cumin, ground ½ t. cloves, ground 1 t. cardamom, ground
3	Add chicken stock and lemon juice and bring to a boil.	2-3 C. chicken stock 1-2 lemons, juiced
4	Stir in the garlic, coconut milk and cream. Simmer uncovered about 15 minutes, stirring frequently until sauce is reduced and thickened.	2 garlic cloves, minced 1 can coconut milk 1 C. crème fraiche
5	Serve over chicken on a bed of basmati rice and toss green onions on top.	4-6 chicken thighs or breasts fully cooked 2-3 green onions, chopped 3 C. basmati rice, cooked

Tip: Serve this dish with a green salad for a complete meal. To lighten this dish, try using lite coconut milk and 2% plain yogurt instead of the crème fraiche.

Chicken with Capers
(Calories: 160, 27 g protein, 5 g fat, 12 g carbohydrates)

Serves 4

1. Sprinkle salt and pepper over chicken.

   4 chicken breast or thighs, boneless, skinless
   ¼ t. sea salt
   ¼ t. pepper
   1 T. olive oil

2. Heat oil in skillet over medium heat. Add chicken and sauté 6 minutes each side or until done. Remove and set aside keeping warm.

3. To skillet; add broth, salt and pepper lemon juice and capers. Stir scraping skillet to loosen brown bits. Cook liquid until reduced to ¼ cup (about 2 minutes).

   ½ C. chicken broth
   3 T. capers, rinsed
   2 T. lemon juice
   ¼ t. sea salt
   ¼ t. pepper

4. Stir in the parsley and spoon over the chicken and serve.

   ¼ C. parsley, chopped

Tip: Serve this with Potato Leek soup or a green salad.

Cauliflower Crust Pizza

Serves 4-6 *Preheat oven to 400°*

½ head cauliflower (aprox. 2 C.)
1 garlic clove, minced
1 C. mozzarella cheese
1 egg, beaten
1 t. basil, dried
1 t. oregano, dried

1 T. olive oil (may use spray)

½ C. Pizza sauce
Your choice of toppings:
Sausage
chicken
Red pepper
Mushroom
Feta cheese
Onion
Spinach
Parmesan cheese

1. Prepare a cookie sheet or a pizza stone. Grease the cookie sheet or use parchment paper. Remove the stems and leaves from the cauliflower and place in blender or food processor and pulse until the texture is like fine rice. Sauté cauliflower over medium heat and cook until it is translucent, about 8 minutes. In a bowl combine the remaining ingredients.

2. Spread dough out evenly over the stone or sheet (if using the sheet you may need to add the olive oil so that it does not stick). The pizza dough should be 9-10 inches in diameter.

3. Bake for 25-30 minutes or until the crust is golden, crispy on the edges and cooked though the middle. Remove from oven and top with pizza sauce and toppings. Broil the pizza for five minutes, allow to cool three minutes and cut and serve immediately.

Tip: This is great served with a large toss green salad.

Rolled Chicken Stuffed with Vegetables

(Calories: 250, 24 g protein, 10 g fat, 16 g carbohydrates)

Serves 4-6

1	In a small sauté pan place balsamic vinegar on medium heat and heat until liquid is reduce ½ the original amount making a reduction. Set aside.	½ C. balsamic vinegar
2	Pound the chicken between two sheets of plastic until ¼ inch thick.	4 boneless, skinless breast or thighs
3	Steam the spinach and drain all water off. If using broccoli; steam florets 5 minutes and remove from steamer, pat dry.	4 oz. of spinach or broccoli
4	Add water to egg and beat until frothy and place in a pie tin. In another pie tin place almond meal, salt and pepper.	1 egg ¼ C. water ½ C. almond meal (may use bread crumbs) ¼ t. sea salt ¼ t. black pepper
5	Place ¼ of the spinach or 1 floret of broccoli on each chicken piece along with 1 t. feta cheese and roll up and secure with pick.	4 oz. goat feta cheese
6	Dip rolled chicken into egg mixture and then into almond meal. Sauté in oil for 10-15 minutes until light brown. Serve drizzled with the balsamic reduction.	

Chicken Crusted in Almonds

(Calories: 150, 28 g protein, 5 g fat, 23g carbohydrates)

Serves 6-8

1	Cut chicken in half and place between two sheets of plastic and pound until ¼ inch thick or twice the original size.	6-8 boneless, skinless chicken breasts or thighs
2	In a pie tin mix together the almond meal, garlic, lemon zest and salt and pepper.	½ C. almond meal 1-2 cloves garlic, minced zest of one organic lemon ¼ t. sea salt ¼ t. pepper
3	In another pie tin crack an egg and whip with a small amount of water until frothy.	1 egg ¼ C. water
4	Heat oil in a large skillet over medium flame and place the chicken dredged in egg and then almond mixture into it. Sauté each side 2-4 minutes until light brown. Serve immediately. Extras can be refrigerated for 2-3 days.	2 T. olive oil or coconut oil

Tip: This served with Sautéed vegetables and a green salad completes the meal.

Turkey Meatloaf

(2 slices: Cal: 335, 20 g protein, 15g fat, 30 g carbohydrates)

Serves 6-8

1	Preheat oven to 375° F.	
2	Rinse the quinoa in a fine mesh under running water. Bring water or broth to a boil and add the quinoa cover and lower to medium heat for 20 minutes. Set aside.	¾ C. organic quinoa 1 ½ C. chicken broth or water
3	Heat oil in large sauté pan and cook onions, carrots, and celery over medium heat for five minutes. Add mushrooms and garlic and cook until moisture is gone about ten minutes. Place meat in a large bowl and mix in the quinoa, vegetables, parsley, eggs, sauce and salt and pepper until just combines. Form into a loaf and roast in the middle of the oven for one hour.	1 T. olive oil ½ onion or shallot, finely chopped 1 carrot, finely chopped 1 large celery rib, finely chopped 5 oz. fresh mushrooms, chopped 2 garlic cloves, finely chopped ½ C., parsley, chopped 2 pounds ground turkey 2 organic eggs 2 T. Worcestershire sauce ½ t. sea salt and pepper
4	Let stand 5 minutes before slicing. May be frozen for 3 months.	

Tip: Use left over quinoa for quicker time.

Stuffed Zucchini
(Calories: 300, 18 g protein, 8 g fat, 39 g carbohydrates)

Serves 6-8

1	Preheat oven to 325° F	
2	Trim the ends off the zucchini, cut in half and scoop out the flesh, keeping ½ for the stuffing but leaving about ¼ inch shell. Sprinkle inside with soy sauce and lemon juice. Bake for 25 minutes. Set aside.	2 extra large zucchini 1 T. tamari wheat free soy sauce 1 T. lemon juice
3	Preheat oven 375° F	
4	Meanwhile make the stuffing: Cook the turkey or ground beef, drain and set aside. In oil cook the vegetables and spices in the order listed. Stir in the zucchini and meat; simmer about ten minutes.	1 lb. ground turkey or beef 1 T. olive oil 1½ C. celery, diced 2 C. onions, diced 1 C. red pepper, chopped 1½ C. tomatoes, seeded and chopped 4 cloves garlic, minced ½ C. sunflower seeds, lightly toasted ¼ C. raisins (optional) 2 t. cumin 1 t. orange peel 1 t. coriander Pinch of sage ¼ t. sea salt and pepper
5	Stuff shells; top with breadcrumbs and cheese. Place on lipped cookie sheet. Pour water on sheet; bake 45 minutes.	¼ C. bread crumbs ¼ C. parmesan cheese ¼ C. water

Chicken Enchiladas

(Calories: 350, 12 g protein, 10 g fat, 50 g carbohydrates)

Serves 8

1	Preheat oven to 375° F	
2	Sauté chicken until done about 5 minutes each side. Or if using a whole chicken place in enough water to cover and simmer for 1 hour. Let cool and skin, debone and shred; set aside.	4-6 chicken breast or thighs or 1 whole chicken
3	Grate zucchini and add chopped green onions to the mixture, set aside.	2-4 zucchini 4-6 green onions, chopped
4	Grate the cheeses, set aside.	3 oz. of cheddar 3 oz. jack cheese
5	Place enchilada sauce in a pan and warm.	1 large can Enchilada sauce (Rosarita or similar)
6	Heat tortillas on the stove until warm.	12-18 corn tortillas
7	Dip the tortilla into the sauce and place in a large baking pan. Add chicken, zucchini mixture and cheese and roll up.	
8	Pour remaining sauce over rolled enchiladas and sprinkle with olives and any remaining cheese. Bake for 15-20 minutes. Freezes well.	1 small can sliced black olives

Fish Marinade

Makes marinade for one pound of fish

1	Combine ingredients and pour over fish.	¼ C. orange juice ¼ C. tamari wheat free soy sauce 1 T. tomato paste 2 T. parsley, chopped 2 T. olive oil 1 T. lemon juice 1 garlic, minced ½ t. oregano leaves, dried ½ t. black pepper
2	Marinade for 1-3 hours.	
3	Grill or broil fish 4-5 minute each side.	

Tip: Marinade fish for 2-3 hours in the refrigerator.

Stacked Halibut and Kale

(Calories: 346, 24 g protein, 10 g fat, 40 g carbohydrates)

Serves 4

1	Preheat broiler to 475° F	
2	Clean, cut in quarters and steam potatoes for 15 minutes. Mash adding butter and half and half until smooth. Season with salt and pepper. Keep warm.	4 C. sweet potatoes 2 T. coconut oil 2 T. coconut cream ¼ t. sea salt ¼ t. pepper
3	Place fish on broiler pan and broil each side 4 minutes.	4 four oz. halibut fillets
4	Steam leaves for 4 minutes; drain.	4 oz. kale leaves
5	On a dinner plate place ¼ of the potatoes in center of plate. Layer with fish and arugula and drizzle with balsamic vinegar. Serve.	balsamic vinegar

Tip: Serve with a green salad.

Salmon Cakes
(Calories: 150, 17 g protein, 7 g fat, 8 g carbohydrates)

Serves 4-6

1	Preheat oven to 400° F	
2	In a food processor process ingredients until minced fine.	½ C. celery ½ C. almond meal ½ C cooked quinoa or wild rice 1/3 C. cilantro ¼ C. onion 1 egg 1 T. Tabasco sauce ¼ t. sea salt ¼ t. pepper
3	Combine the salmon with the mixture and form into patties on waxed paper and chill for 30 minutes.	1 lb. cooked salmon, diced
4	Heat oil in skillet over medium heat. Cook the patties about 2-3 minutes per side. Transfer to oven and cook through about 4 minutes. Serve immediately.	1-2 T. olive oil or coconut oil

Tip: These are great served over a large green salad.

Greek Stuffed Steak

(Calories: 177, 21 g protein, 8 g fat, 4 g carbohydrate)

Serves 4-6

1 Combine in a bowl; set aside

- 1 (10 oz.) frozen spinach, thawed, drained
- 1/3 C. red onion, chopped
- 1/3 C. pepperoncini peppers, chopped
- 2 T. breadcrumbs
- ¼ t. garlic powder
- 4 oz. feta cheese
- 1½ lb. flank steak (grass-fed if possible)

2 Trim the fat off the steak. Cut horizontally through center of steak, cutting to, but not through other side; open flat as you would a book. Place steak between two sheets of plastic; flatten to an even thickness, using a meat mallet or rolling pin.

3 Spread spinach mixture over steak leaving a 1 inch margin around outside edges. Roll up jelly roll fashion and secure with heavy cooking string.

4 Coat a large Dutch oven with oil and place over medium high heat. Brown steak well on all sides. Add wine, broth, and oregano to pan; bring to a boil. Cover and reduce heat and simmer 1 ½ hours until tender, turning meat once. Add additional water during cooking if needed. Remove string and cut steak into 8 slices.

- 2 T. olive oil
- ½ C. dry red wine
- 1 (14 ½ ounce) can beef broth
- ½ t. oregano, dried
- ½ C. water (if needed)

Tip: Serve with Potato Leek soup and a green salad.

Greek Moussaka

(Calories: 340, 15 g protein, 22 g fat, 20 g carbohydrates)

Serves 8

1	Preheat oven to 450° F	
2	Peel eggplant and cut into slices ¼ inch thick. Brush with olive oil and bake for 10 minutes turning once.	3 large eggplant ¼ C. olive oil
3	Heat butter and oil; add onion, garlic and cook 3 minutes.	2 T. butter 2 T. olive oil 2 C. onion, diced 1-2 cloves garlic, minced
4	Add meat and cook until browned about 5-10 minutes. Drain off fat.	2 lb. ground turkey
5	Stir in tomato paste, puree, wine and spices; simmer until almost dry about 30 minutes.	3 T. tomato paste ½ C. tomato puree ½ C. dry red wine ½ t. cinnamon 1 t. oregano, dried
6	To make white sauce melt oil and add flour and milk stirring constantly until thick; remove from heat and stir in eggs, nutmeg, parsley and ricotta cheese.	¼ C. coconut oil 3 T. quinoa flour 2 C. almond milk 2 eggs, lightly whipped ½ T. nutmeg, freshly ground ½ C. parsley, chopped 1 C. ricotta cheese
7	Grease a 3-quart casserole and sprinkle with bread crumbs. Arrange layers with eggplant, parmesan cheese and meat. Pour the white sauce on top.	½ C. almond meal
8	Bake in a 350° oven for one hour.	May be refrigerated for 4 days or frozen for 3 months.

Tip: This should be served with a large green salad with cucumbers, tomatoes and oil and vinegar dressing.

Bacon-Wrapped Pork Tenderloin Filets

(Calories: 280, 22 g protein, 20 g fat, 5g carbohydrates)

Serves 4

1	Prepare pork: Trim off silver skin and fat and cut into 2" thick filets. Prepare the grill on medium high.	2 pork tenderloins (1 ½ lb. each)
2	To make the Chimichurri sauce; mince in food processor until smooth the first four ingredients and then add the oil, vinegar and water. Set aside ¼ C. for serving.	2 C. parsley leaves 2 T. garlic, chopped ½ t. pepper ½ t. red pepper flakes ½ C. olive oil ¼ C. white balsamic vinegar 2 T. water 12 strips bacon, thin
3	Wrap bacon strips around each filet overlapping the ends and skewer each filet. Brush with Chimichurri sauce.	
4	Grill each side turning every 4 minutes basting with sauce each turn. Grill until internal temperature reaches 145° F, about 15 minutes. Serve with extra sauce.	

Tip: This works well with the Quinoa Corn Salad.

Chipotle-Marinated Pork Tenderloin

(Calories: 140, 24 g protein, 4 g fat, 2 g carbohydrates)

Serves 4

1. In a food processor or blender combine and set aside.

   - 1 small can chipotle peppers in adobo sauce
   - 1 garlic clove, chopped
   - 1/3 C. orange juice
   - 3 T. lime juice
   - 1 T. apple cider vinegar
   - ¼ t. cumin
   - 1 t. oregano, dried
   - ¼ t. sea salt
   - ¼ t. pepper
   - 2 eight oz. pork tenderloins

2. Place pork tenderloins in plastic bag with sauce and marinate for at least 1 hour.

3. Preheat grill to high heat. Remove the pork from the bag. Grill turning every 4-5 minutes for 15-20 minutes or until the instant-read thermometer reads 145° F.

4. Transfer pork to cutting board and let sit before slicing.

Tip: This recipe can be used cold sliced on greens with sliced fennel, orange segments and topped with pumpkin seeds. Drizzle with oil and vinegar dressing.

Pear and Cranberry Stuffed Pork Roast
(Calories: 170, 19 g protein, 7 g fat, 8 g carbohydrates)

Serves 4-6

1 Preheat oven to 400° F

2 Heat oil in a large skillet over medium heat. Add onions, thyme, sage and garlic: sauté for 2 minutes until onion is tender. Stir in the broth scrapping the pan to loosen the brown bits. Cook until liquid is almost evaporated about 5 minutes.

1 T. olive oil
¼ C. onion diced
½ t. thyme, dried
½ t. sage. dried
2 cloves garlic, minced
½ C. chicken broth

3 Add the pear; cooking 5 minutes stirring often. Add cranberries and apple juice and cook 5 minutes. Remove from heat; let cool.

1½ C. pear, chopped
¼ C. dried cranberries
¼ C. apple juice

4 Spread Pork out; sprinkle with salt and pepper. Spread pear mixture over roast leaving 2 inch margins around edges. Roll up jelly roll style securing with twine. Bake at 400° for 15 minutes.

2-3 lb. pork tenderloin roast

5 Reduce temperature to 325° and cook for 1 hour or until the thermometer reads 160°F.

6 Let stand for 10 minutes before slicing.

Spanish Paella

(Calories: 355, 20 g protein, 12 g fat, 48 g carbohydrates)

Serves 8-10

1	Combine saffron and broth in a saucepan. Bring to a boil and then lower flame; set aside. Make Herb blend by combining parsley, lemon juice, olive oil and garlic and set aside.	1 T. saffron threads 1 quart chicken broth 1 C. parsley, chopped ¼ C. lemon juice 2 T. olive oil 2 cloves garlic, minced
2	Heat oil in large skillet over medium heat and add chicken; sauté on both side 4 minutes and remove from pan.	2 T. olive oil 4 chicken thighs, boned and skinned
3	Add sausage and sauté 2 minutes; remove from pan.	7 pork sausages
4	Add shrimp and sauté 2 minutes and remove from pan.	½ lb. shrimp, peeled, tails on
5	Reduce heat to medium and add onion and peppers; sauté 15 minutes.	2 C. onion, chopped 1 C. red bell peppers, chopped
6	Add tomatoes, paprika and garlic; cook 5 minutes. Add rice and cook 1 minute stirring. Add herb blend, broth mixture, chicken, sausage and cook 5 minutes.	1 C. tomatoes, diced 1 t. paprika 3 cloves garlic 4 C. cooked brown rice
7	Add shrimp and cook 5 minutes.	
8	Sprinkle with lemon juice. Remove from heat and serve.	¼ C. lemon juice

Desserts and Snacks
May have on occasion

Pear Apple Crisp

(Calories: 200, 4 g protein, 4 g fat, 38 g carbohydrates)

Serves 12

1	Preheat oven to 400° F	
2	To make filling combine in a 2-quart baking dish all ingredients and set aside.	1 lb. organic apples. thinly sliced 1 lb. organic pears, thinly sliced 1 T. lemon juice ½ T. stevia (may use 2 T. maple syrup) 1 t. vanilla extract 1 T. arrowroot powder 1 t. cinnamon ½ C. organic unsweetened apple juice
3	To make the topping mix ingredients well and pour over filling.	½ C. coconut flakes, unsweetened ½ C. almond meal ¼ C. coconut oil (liquefied) ¼ t. stevia or 1 T. maple syrup 1 C. toasted walnuts, chopped
4	Cover dish with foil and bake for 45 minutes. Uncover and continue baking until golden brown about 20 minutes.	
5	May be eaten warm or at room temperature.	

Tip: Serve with a tablespoon of yogurt (see recipe for Yogurt Dessert) on top.

Energy Trail Mix for #1-O

(1/4 cup serving: Calories 200, 9 g protein, 18 g fat, 18 g carbohydrates)

Serves 26

1 In a medium size bowl....

　　Mix all the ingredients.

½ C. dried wild blueberries
1 C. *coca nibs
1 C. almonds, whole, raw
1 C. cashews, whole, raw
1 C. hulled raw sunflower seeds
1 C. walnuts
1 C. pumpkin seeds raw
May add:
½ t. stevia or ½ T. maple sprinkles
¼ t. sea salt

*cocoa nibs can be used in recipes or for a snack when chocolate taste buds need satisfying. May be found at your health food store.

2 Store in a covered jar and keep in a dark place or refrigerate.

Raspberry-Rhubarb Pie
(Calories: 250, 47 g protein, 8 g fat, 40 g carbohydrates)

Serves 6-8

1	Preheat oven to 350° F	
2	Place tapioca in a coffee grinder or spice grinder; process until finely ground.	2 t. uncooked tapioca
3	Combine tapioca with ingredients in a bowl and let stand 10 minutes.	4½ C. fresh raspberries (aprox. 24 oz.) 3½ C. chopped fresh rhubarb (about 6 stalks) ¼ C. maple syrup (or use 1 T. stevia) ¼ C. cornstarch ¼ C. apple juice pinch sea salt
4	To make the crust combine *Berry good cereal, nuts and coconut oil in a food processor and process until paste is formed. Place in the bottom of a lightly oiled pie pan and gently press the dough into the pie dish. Bake 10 minutes.	2 C. *Berry Good Cereal (may use ½ C. sunflower seeds, ½ C. walnuts, ½ C. oats, 1 t. stevia) ½ C. almonds ¼ C. coconut oil liquefied
5	Spoon raspberry mixture into crust and bake 40 minutes.	
6	While pie bakes, combine cereal or nuts, flour and sweetener in a food processor; pulse 10 times until mixture resembles coarse crumbs.	¼ C. Berry Good Cereal or almonds 1 t. stevia or **maple sprinkles 5 T. coconut flour (may use quinoa flour)
7	Increase oven temperature to 375° and sprinkle topping over pie. Bake 15 minutes more. Cool before serving.	

*See resources for Lydia Organic Berry Good Cereal
**Shady Maple Farms from www.citadelle-camp.coop.com

Nancy's New Energy Cookies

(Calories: 250, 10 g protein, 15 g fat, 18 g carbohydrates)

Makes 36-48 cookies

1	Preheat oven to 350° F	
2	Mix dry ingredients in a large bowl. Set aside.	3 C.* organic quinoa flour ½ C. Stevia baking blend (NuStevia brand) 1 t. salt 2 t. baking powder 1 C. pumpkin seeds 1 C. sesame seeds 1 C. walnut pieces 2 C. semi-sweet chocolate chips (65% chocolate)
3	Beat almond butter, coconut oil until creamy; add eggs and vanilla extract.	1 C. almond butter 3 organic large eggs ¾ C. coconut oil, heated to liquid 2 t. vanilla extract
4	Mix wet into dry ingredients. Batter should be stiff yet moist. Mix in currants and the hot water. Use more water if needed.	1 C. currants (soaked in hot water)
5	Using a spoon form cookies and place on a cookie sheet. Flatten cookies slightly.	
6	Bake 20 minutes or until golden around the edges.	Store in refrigerator for 5 days in airtight container or freeze for 3-4 months.

Tip: * May grind your own using organic quinoa and store in airtight container in refrigerator.

Banana Cashew Slice

(Calories: 120, 2 g protein, 5 g fat, 17 g carbohydrates)

Serves 6-8

1	Preheat oven to 375° F	
2	Blend in food processor or blender.	¼ C. coconut oil, warmed to liquid 2 medium bananas ½ t vanilla extract 1 t. cinnamon ¼ t. cardamom
3	Add to mixture and blend.	½ C. cashews
4	Add to mixture and blend.	1 C. dry unsweetened coconut flakes ½ C. quinoa flour 1 apple, grated
5	Pour into a greased 9 inch baking pan. Bake for 25-30 minutes.	
6	Cool; cut into wedges.	

Tip: Top with plain yogurt or whipped cream (sweetened with stevia and vanilla extract) and sprinkle toasted unsweetened coconut flakes.

Mango Frozen Yogurt
(Serving 1/2 cup 98 calories, 4 g protein, 2 g fat, 16 g carbohydrates)

Serves 4

1	Mix together in a bowl.	4 C. plain yogurt (Fage 2% or similar) 1 T. stevia or 2-3 T honey 1 t. vanilla extract
2	Mix the milk into the yogurt.	¾ C. whole organic milk
3	Thaw mango pieces and add to mixture using a blender or hand mixer, blend until smooth.	16 oz. of frozen mango pieces
4	Pour into an ice cream maker and mix until thickened about 20-25 minutes.	
5	Spoon into cups and garnish with a mint leaf.	mint leaves

Tip: You can use frozen peaches or strawberries in place of the mango for a different flavor.

Yogurt Dessert
Ricotta Cheese Dessert

Serves 4-6

1. **Yogurt Dessert**

    In bowl mix yogurt with stevia and vanilla extract until smooth.

    In 4-6 custard cups place ½ cup chopped berries top with ½ cup yogurt mixture and sprinkle with ½ T toasted nuts, serve.

    - 15 oz. Greek plain yogurt (Fage 2% or full fat)
    - 1 T. stevia powder or 2-3 T honey
    - 1 t. vanilla extract
    - 1 lb. fresh berries
    - ¼ C. chopped nuts, toasted

2. **Ricotta Cheese Dessert**

    Mix ricotta in bowl with stevia or honey and vanilla.

    Grate the chocolate and gentle fold into cheese mixture.

    Place ½ cup in small cup or glass and top with a macaroon cookie.

    - 1 pt. ricotta cheese
    - 1 T. stevia or 2-3 T honey
    - 1 t. vanilla extract
    - 1 squares 72% dark chocolate
    - 4-6 macaroon cookies

Tip: Fage yogurt is a Greek style thick yogurt that can be found locally or through www.fageusa.com

Glossary

Arrowroot: A white powder used for thickening sauces. It becomes clear when cooked.

Arugula (Rocket Rugula): An elongated green leaf with a peppery sharp almost mustardy flavor. It can be used in place of spinach in soups and vegetables stews.

Barley: An ancient grain that is very digestible. Hulled barley is superior over pearl barley but it requires longer cooking time and is chewier.

Bragg Liquid Aminos: This is a very tasty soy sauce-like condiment made by extracting amino acids from organic soybeans. It is not fermented, making it an ideal seasoning for those who suffer from yeast sensitivities. You can find it in most health food stores.

Capers: Pickled flower buds. Adds a salty taste; always rinse before using.

Coconut oil: It is a saturated fat that cooks at high temperatures without smoking.

Couscous: A staple of North Africa is made of durum wheat stripped of the bran and germ. Try and get whole wheat couscous which has the bran. It is very quick to cook in less than five minutes.

Curry Paste: A concentrated seasoned mixture of red chilies and spices found in oriental and eastern foods. It can be very hot.

Curry Powder: A blend of spices with degrees of "heat" from maker to maker. Most curry powders have the following: cumin, coriander, mustard seeds, fenugreek, red chilies, black pepper, and turmeric.

Cardamom: A spice found in curry powders. It adds a sweet-spiciness to baked goods and cuts through the flavor and texture of oil.

Fennel: Has a sweet licorice taste. The plant looks like celery. Sliced in salads or soups it adds a delicate taste. I prefer the fennel raw or I like to add at the end of the dish to retain the flavor.

Fish Sauce: Made from salted anchovies. May use in place of salt or soy sauce. It has a very pungent aroma, but the aroma will mellow with cooking.

Flax Seeds: Have a high omega-3 fatty acid ratio and make for a good binder in baked goods. They have a sweet nutty flavor. Because of their high oil content, the seeds tend to go rancid. Store them whole in the freezer for up to three months and grind as needed. They have a laxative effect so eat flax in moderation.

Garam Masala: A blend of dry roasted spices used in Indian cooking. Combination of about twelve spices including: black pepper, cinnamon, cloves, coriander, cumin, fennel, mace and nutmeg. Add towards the end of cooking for more flavors.

Ghee: Clarified butter used in Indian and Middle Eastern cooking. It can be made by melting unsalted butter and removing the scum and foam from the top as it melts.

Ginger, fresh: Buy ginger fresh with smooth skin and store in your refrigerator in a brown bag sealed tightly. To use the root cut a piece and grate or slice. It is not necessary to peel the root unless it is dark brown and shriveled. It should have plenty of juice which can be added to the dish as well. If the recipe calls for fresh ginger you can not substitute dried as it has an entirely different flavor.

Goatein protein powder: A protein powder made from pre-digested goats milk. Made by Garden of Life.

Gomasio: Ground sesame seeds and sea salt.

Great Northern Beans: These are white beans harvested in the Mid-west.

Hemp protein powder: Contains all essential amino acids along with a balance of omega 6 and omega 3 in a ratio of 3 to 1. It also contains GLA for hormone balancing.

Lentils: A very ancient legume. There are many varieties. Brown have a peppery taste, green have a milder taste and my favorite are the French variety that are smaller, sweeter and hold its shape in soups and salads.

Quinoa: Native grain from the Andes and about the size of a sesame seed. Has higher protein and amino acid profile. Be sure and rinse well to remove the bitter saponin coating (believed to be a natural insect repellant) before cooking and drain it thoroughly.

Rhubarb: Considered a fruit it is really a vegetable with red stalks and poisonous leaves. Select medium–thick stalks to slender so they are less stringy; can be stored in the refrigerator for one week sealed in a plastic bag. For cooking rinse well and cut off the ends and slice as directed.

Sea salt: Evaporated seawater which leaves trace minerals lost in refined salt. Has less sodium.

Soba Noodles: Buckwheat noodles. Generally, have other ingredients. I prefer the Eden Foods' brand. The Japanese technique of adding ½ cup of cold water to the boiling water twice during cooking time allows the middle of the noodle to cook thoroughly before the outside becomes soft and mushy.

Spelt: An ancient grain with a texture very similar to wheat. Some people who have sensitivity to wheat may be able to tolerate spelt.

Stevia: Natural sweetener from a plant grown in South America. It is ten times sweeter than sugar so use less.

Tamari: Type of naturally fermented soy sauce that takes a year to ferment. I prefer the organic wheat free type.

Tahini: Sesame butter; a rich peanut-buttery paste used in Middle Eastern and Asian cooking.

Tobasco Sauce: A well known brand name of a hot sauce used in vegetable or meat dishes.

Whey protein powder: Lactose free protein made from cow dairy. Use only good quality without any other ingredients or additives.

Legends, Weights and Measures

pinch = less then ¼ teaspoon
t.= teaspoon
T.= Tablespoon
C. = Cup
oz. = ounce
pt. = pint
lb. = pound
qt. = quart

To convert to metric

1 Cup = 250 ml
1 Tablespoon = 15 ml (Australia it would be 20 ml)
1 teaspoon = 5 ml

Oven setting equivalents

	Fahrenheit	Celsius	Gas regulo No
Very cool	225-275°	110-140	¼-1
Cool	300-325°	150-160	2-3
Moderate	350-375°	180-190	4-5
Hot	400-450°	200-260	6-8
Very Hot	475-500°	250-260	9-10

Grams to Ounces: These are converted to the nearest round number.

25=1	50=2	75=3	100=3.5	125=4	150=5
175=6	200=7	225=8	250=9	275=10	300=10.5
325=11	350=12	400=14	425=15	450=16	

1 kilogram= 1000 grams= 2lb. 4 oz.

Index

Apples
    Almond Pancakes, 20
    Pear Apple Crisp, 102
Bacon
    Ratatouille, 72
    Bacon-wrapped Pork Tenderloin Filets, 95
Banana
    Protein Smoothies, 28
    Banana coconut flour Nut Muffins, 21
    Banana Cashew Slice, 108
Beans,
    Black Bean, Corn and Red Pepper Salad, 36
    Black Bean Soup, 52
    Black Bean Chili, 54
    Hummus, 41
    White Bean Chili, 55
    Chicken and Spinach Soup with Fresh Pesto, 56
Beef
    Greek Stuffed Steak, 93
    Black Bean Chili, 54
Blueberry
    Protein Smoothies, 28
    Yogurt Dessert, 111
Broccoli
    Rolled Chicken Stuffed with Vegetables, 83
Chicken
    Chicken Suma Salad, 34
    Chicken Bone Broth, 47
    Chicken and Spinach Soup, 56
    Chicken Crusted in Almond, 84
    Chicken Curry, 80
    Chicken with Capers, 81
    Orange-ginger Chicken, 77
    Chicken Enchiladas, 88
    Rolled Chicken Stuffed with Vegetables, 83
    Grilled Chicken with Papaya Salsa, 78
    Spanish Paella, 98
Desserts
    Banana Cashew Slice, 108
    Energy Cookies, 106
    Energy Trail Mix, 103
    Mango Frozen Dessert, 110
    Pear Apple Crisp, 102
    Raspberry-Rhubarb Pie, 104
    Ricotta Cheese Dessert, 111
    Yogurt Dessert, 111
Eggs
    Egg white Frittata, 22
    Salmon Omelet, 24
Fish
    Ceviche, 38
    Ciopino, 61

Salmon Omelet, 24
Stacked Halibut and Arugula, 91
Salmon Cakes, 92
Spanish Paella, 98
Fish Marinade, 90

Muffins
- Banana Coconut Flour Muffins, 21
- Nancy's No-Carb Zucchini Muffins, 26
- Zucchini Muffins, 25

Nuts and Seeds
- Energy Trail Mix, 103

Onion
- Baked Stuffed Onion, 71

Pancakes
- Almond Pancakes, 20

Pears
- Pear and Walnut Green Salad, 32
- Pear and Cranberry Stuffed Pork Roast, 97
- Pear Apple Crisp, 102

Pork
- Bacon-wrapped Pork Tenderloin Filets, 95
- Pear and Cranberry Stuffed Pork Roast, 97
- Chipotle-Marinated Pork Tenderloin, 96

Potato
- Potato Leek Soup, 60
- Twice Baked Potatoes, 68

Ratatouille, 72

Raspberry
- Raspberry-Rhubarb Pie, 104
- Protein Smoothie, 28

Salads
- Black Bean, Corn and Red Pepper Salad, 36
- Chicken Suma Salad, 34
- Fresh Fig Salad with Toasted Walnuts, 33
- Lentil Salad, 40
- Pear Walnut Green Salad, 32
- Quinoa Corn Salad, 35

Salmon
- Salmon Omelet, 24
- Salmon Cakes, 92

Shrimp
- Spanish Paella, 98
- Cioppino, 38

Smoothies
- Basic berry, 28
- Creamy monkey, 28
- Reese's pieces, 28
- Tropical delight, 28
- Raspberry delight, 28

Sausage
- Nancy's Spiced Greens and Sausage, 76
- Spanish Paella, 98

Soups
- Black Bean, 52

Bone Broth, 47
Butternut, 50
Chicken Bone Broth, 47
Chicken and Spinach, 56
Chilled Cantaloupe, 65
Cleansing Broth, 49
Cioppino, 61
Creamy Potato and Greens, 59
Fennel and Lemon, 64
Italian Vegetable with Chicken, 58
Lentil Vegetable, 51
Potato Leek, 60
Roasted Pumpkin, 62
Vegetable Broth, 46

Turkey
Black Bean Chili, 54
Greek Moussaka, 94
White Bean Chili, 55
Stuffed Zucchini, 87
Nancy's Spiced Greens and Sausage, 76
Turkey Meatloaf, 86

Vegetables
Crust less Spinach Pie, 69
Mediterranean Vegetable Quinoa, 70
Ratatouille, 72
Stuffed Zucchini, 87
Twice Baked Potato, 68

Resources

US Wellness Meats
Grass fed beef, lamb, bison and free range poultry online store: (877) 383-0051
www.uswellnessmeats.com

Great Alaska Seafood
Wild caught seafood delivered to your door. (866) 262-8846
www.great-alaskan-seafood.com

Tropical Traditions
Organic Coconut oil and Flour and other items. Mail order to: P.O. Box 333, Springville, CA. 93265
www.tropicaltraditions.com

Lydia's Organics
Vegan-Gluten Free-Raw snacks. Phone: 415-258-9678 Fax: 415-258-9623
Convenient alternatives to commercial snacks, crackers, cereals and bars.
www.lydiaorganics.com

Julian Bakery
Organic wheat-free, preservative free breads. Phone 1-800-98-BREAD
www.julianbakery.com

Ultra-Life/Synergistics
Supplements , Celtic Salt, household and Miscellaneous Phone: 800-323-3842 Fax: 618-594-7712
www.ultralifeinc.com

Nan Tucket Rubs and Spices
Rubs and spices
www.nantucketoffshore.com

La Nogalera Walnut Oil
Walnut oil
www.langalerawalnutoil.com

Shady Maple Farms
Maple syrup products and farm co-op
www.citadelle-camp.coop.com

www.ingramcontent.com/pod-product-compliance
Lightning Source LLC
Chambersburg PA
CBHW041548220426
43665CB00003B/60